How to Get Your TED Talk Banned

(and other lessons in public speaking)

Peter Sandbach

Peter Sandbach
Visit my website at http://freerangecommunications.com

First Printing: May 2018

ISBN 978-19-80586-10-4

For my mum, who always knew right from wrong, and would never keep silent if she experienced the latter.

CONTENTS

Foreword...2

PART I: How to Get Your TED Talk Banned 4

Introduction 5

Chapter 1: Meet the Freaks..6

Chapter 2: Getting It On 9

Chapter 3: Foreplay..12

Chapter 4: Climax 16

Chapter 5: Afterglow 18

Chapter 6: Bombshell...22

Chapter 7: Let Battle Commence 25

Chapter 8: Fighting the Good Fight....................................27

Chapter 9: Rallying the Troops 30

Chapter 10: The Empire Strikes Back 32

Chapter 11: The Last Straw...34

Chapter 12: The Phoenix Rises 37

Chapter 13: The Final Blows 39

Chapter 14: Enough Is Enough...41

Chapter 15: Fame at Last 43

Epilogue: Lessons Learned 45

A cure for corporate jargon...47

PART II: and other lessons in public speaking...................52

Public Speaking Lesson 1: Why You?.................................53

Public Speaking Lesson 2: It's Not About YOU................55

Public Speaking Lesson 3: Be Yourself..............................57

Public Speaking Lesson 4: Always Be Prepared................59

Public Speaking Lesson 5: Don't Be a PowerPoint Slave 61

Public Speaking Lesson 6: Give Yourself a Chance 63

Public Speaking Lesson 7: Build a Connection..................65

Public Speaking Lesson 8: Don't Try to Be Too Clever......67

Public Speaking Lesson 9: Tell Stories 69

Public Speaking Lesson 10: Find Out How You Did 71

About the Author...72

FOREWORD

BY MARTY HIRSCH

THIS BOOK IS NOT FOR EVERYBODY. Not everybody will be interested in the subject, effective public speaking and unfettered free speech. And not everybody will be sympathetic to the actions of the author, who went further than most would to say exactly what he wanted to say in a public forum and circulate a video of his performance afterward, even to the point of breaking or at least bending some rules.

But I'm not everybody, and neither is Peter Sandbach. So when he asked me to write the foreword to his book, I agreed without hesitation. I agreed in spite of the fact that many of Peter's friends and colleagues fiercely believe he's walking a foolhardy and risky path that could be damaging to his fledgling communications consulting business, because it could alienate potential corporate clients who might find his boat-rocking outspokenness excessive.

As close as I am to Peter and the experiences that drove him to write this book, I really don't know what made him such a warrior for free speech and expression. His situation, though, made me ponder my own evolution as corporate communications revolutionary. The search through my memory bank led me all the way back to 1962.

I was 11 at the time, and my father took me to the movies to see Tarus Bulba – a tale of the wars between the Cossacks and the Poles starring Yul Brynner and Tony Curtis. In a scene that gripped my little boy's heart and left its mark on my mind for life, a massive Cossack marauder roughhousing with the Tony Curtis character at a raucous party got into a tiff with him and called him a coward. The circus-like scene stopped on a dime and things got deadly serious. Calling someone a coward meant they'd have to meet at a great, gaping gorge at dawn and gallop their horses over the ominous cliff, back and forth, until one of them didn't make it to the other side. When the actress playing Curtis's mother pleaded to her husband to cancel the contest she feared would end her son's life, crying that it was only over words, Yul Brynner said with a baleful glare, "There are some words men must die for".

Yes, it was dramatic and over the top, in that inimitable golden-age-of-Hollywood way. But it stuck with me, and I've always been inclined, as if by some quirk in my genetics, to fight for words: that the right ones be used, that they be clear and precise, that they be honest and true, and most of all, that they be uncensored. At its core, that's what Peter's book is about. And that's why I endorse it.

When Peter and I worked in corporate communications together, we put forward a manifesto whose core tenets included credibility, achieved by balanced and objective communications not compromised by spin, free of jargon and explaining things in their full context, even if that means raising the curtain on sensitive or controversial but substantively relevant facts.

It was part of what we called a communications revolution, one which our boss actually went along with, at least for a while. Walking this line has its risks, and they get higher the farther you tread and with every rung you climb up the corporate ladder.

In the spirit of our revolution and its manifesto, Peter prepared a talk on the scourge of corporate-speak and gave his all to presenting it at a TEDxBasel event. In the 11-minute presentation, he used the word "bullshit" exactly one time, because it was the precise word that conveyed the precise meaning in precisely the right tone for the message that was the core of his speech. The audience loved it and the feedback was phenomenal.

However, the event organisers refused to publish his talk. Peter had defied their stated preference for the substitution of that word. In fairness, some may say that Peter is at least partly to blame for the acrimonious dispute that constitutes the basis of this book. And given that every story has two sides, Peter's detractors have their points of view and are entitled to their opinions.

Mine is that Peter indeed went further than most would to fight his adversaries tooth and nail and then some, that it would have been a lot easier and probably more prudent, too, to simply put this matter behind him, but that, at the same time, "there are some words men must die for", or at least take a strong and principled stand on.

That's what Peter did. And I applaud him for it.

PART I

How to Get Your TED Talk Banned

INTRODUCTION

"Next time, could you try it without using the word *bullshit?*", asked Jane, after listening to one of my final rehearsals.

Jane was one of the main organisers of the event where I was about to make one of the most important – and life-changing – speeches of my life.

"Can I ask why?", I enquired.

"Well, we are teachers and we like to show the talks to our classes at school. If you use that word, we can't show it. Besides that, when your talk is published online, you will miss out on hits from American audiences if you use *that* word", she answered.

"But my talk is about bullshit. It would seem odd not to name it. And I wrote it for an audience of adults, not schoolchildren."

"Just try saying *B.S.* instead. It'll be just the same", came the response.

At that point I didn't give a moment's thought to the consequences of using one seemingly-innocuous word: *bullshit.* But use it I did, and I suffered the consequences. My talk was banned.

This book tells the story of how doing an 11-minute TED[1] talk changed my perspective of myself and other people, almost got me slammed up in jail, and could have cost me my job. As well as lessons learned from this experience, in the second section of this book I'll give public speaking tips from my many years as a communication trainer.

---

[1] TED: Technology, Entertainment and Design is a non-profit organisation devoted to spreading ideas. More later.

CHAPTER 1

Meet the Freaks

I've always been one of those weird people who get a kick out of speaking in public. Perhaps it was my way to become famous. At the age of fourteen, my five-minute speech about zip fasteners took me to the dizzying heights of the Buxton Opera House for the North-West England regional finals of *Youth Speaks*, a competition run by the Rotary Club. Leftwich High School's 1987 dream team of Sarah, Ruth, and I were narrowly beaten by three posh girls from Altrincham who spoke about France. I guess the judges didn't consider a podgy blond kid with a broad Cheshire accent talking on the topic of zip fasteners quite high-brow enough.

So, many years later, when I received a call in the winter of 2015 from my friend Martin Daubney asking if I would consider talking at TEDxBasel, I immediately said yes, without giving it a moment's consideration. TED (Technology, Entertainment and Design) is a non-profit organisation that is "devoted to spreading ideas". This is usually in the form of short, powerful talks, which have become incredibly popular online in recent years. TED holds global conferences and provides licences for independently-run TEDx events in communities around the world.

I had watched many TED talks in my capacity as a communication trainer and used some in my training courses. I had long admired thought-provoking and entertaining TED speakers such as Sir Ken Robinson and Benjamin Zander, whose online views number in the millions.

"We'd like you to do a three-minute funny spot", said Martin, "a kind of palate cleanser at the event". Martin was on the organising committee of TEDxBasel. TEDx events are independently organised, with the US-based TED organisation granting licences for volunteers to set up local events under certain rules. Basel is tucked into the North-West corner of Switzerland and has an active community of English-speaking expats, of which I have been a member since 2001.

I started thinking about the topic I might tackle for a "three-minute funny spot". I'm no stand-up comedian so hadn't a routine already prepared. Ever since the zip fastener runner-up incident, I've always said it's far better to talk about something you know well. Having worked in communications for twenty-odd years, mainly within large corporations, I decided to tackle the topic of pompous, deliberately baffling language used by self-important people in the business world. I know many such people and have plenty of examples. I had no qualms about a polished delivery, with countless Master of Ceremonies and corporate event moderation jobs under my belt.

I started writing some notes on the back of an empty cigarette packet during a smoke break and the beginnings of my idea for a speech were forming.

Martin had arranged an audition for me in front of the lead organisers of TEDxBasel, Harrison and Jane[2].

It was a wintry evening in a meeting room they had commandeered from the Legal Department of Basel University. I felt the nerves building up inside me as I smoked my last cigarette before going into the building with my embryonic ideas on the back of a cigarette packet. Inside, I explained the concept for my "palate cleanser" to Harrison and Jane.

They must've been amused by my first ideas because a few days later Martin called to invite me to the first TEDxBasel wannabe speakers' meeting. This took place on a frozen January evening in the top-floor meeting room of a former factory in the trendy post-industrial area of Basel. Around nine other TEDx hopefuls were at the event, including a colleague from the company I then worked for.

It was an evening of exchanging pleasantries with the other potential speakers and being briefed by Harrison and Jane on the formidable TED process they were about to take us through. It would all start with "the idea", which they and their volunteer coaches would help us to develop, right through to reciting our speech in front of 700 people at Basel's Musical Theatre that coming May.

There was a sharp gasp from everyone when Jane projected a picture of the Musical Theatre seen from the stage outwards, its rows of empty red seats striking fear and excitement into this group of would-be performers. I doubt any of us had ever been on

---

[2] Not their real names. You will see why I am not including their real names as the story unfolds.

stage at such a prestigious venue before, except, of course, for me at the Buxton Opera House.

CHAPTER 2

Getting It On

I was pleased to learn that my coach would be Martin. I knew he'd be honest with his feedback. He'd tell me what works and what doesn't. We all need to know what we're doing well because sometimes we get obsessed with our own faults. That said, we do need to know what's not working. As another trainer I work with puts it: "It's the poppy seed effect. If you're at a cocktail party and you eat one of those canapés with black seeds on top, then have a poppy seed stuck in your teeth, you'd rather someone told you than smile at everyone all evening with it."

Martin and I got together several times to flesh out my idea of "piercing the pomposity of people who take themselves too seriously". By now, we had realised that this topic couldn't be tackled adequately in a three-minute "palate cleanser" spot, and Jane and Harrison agreed to upgrade me to a full speaking slot. The TED guidelines state that 18 minutes is the maximum length for a standard talk, but in recent years they've discovered that less is more in terms of online views. I was allocated 11 minutes by TEDxBasel.

I had already been through several drafts of the speech by the date all speakers had been instructed to submit their scripts. The speeches would then be vetted and edited by the two people at the head of TEDxBasel, something I'd not expected from an organisation affiliated with TED, which is devoted to "spreading ideas". You don't imagine anyone taking a red pen to Al Gore.

By this time, I had already decided to put aside my pre-conceived ideas as a communication and presentation trainer myself. This time, I would take on the TED experience from the inside, as a speaker. I reckoned that immersing myself in the process the TEDxBasel organisers were about to put me through would be a learning experience for me as a speaker, as well as a trainer afterwards.

I was on my way to a friend's *Eurovision* night when I had an appointment at Jane and Harrison's apartment in the trendiest area of Basel to go through the latest version of the script and decide on the final direction of the talk. They gave me some feedback and the three of us came up with some further ways of developing the talk. Overall they were pleased with how it was progressing.

After a couple more sessions with Martin, my script was shaping up well. I had dropped one of the initial concepts that seemed to be constricting the shape of the talk, as well as one or two anecdotes that were taking up time but not adding to the idea. Here's one:

My ten-year-old daughter is a fabulous literal thinker. I once asked her "Patti, if frankfurters are from Frankfurt, and hamburgers are from Hamburg, where is Wiener Schnitzel from?" She thought for a moment and then said "Venus?"

Every sentence matters when you have a limited time to talk, and even though a tale like that might get an audience to smile, you need to be ruthless with your words.

I've mentioned the importance of getting feedback so that you can uncover blind spots and amplify strong points. I'd decided that my talk was now in such an advanced stage as to be tested on a virgin audience, one who had not yet been exposed to my speech at all.

I'd been running a series of presentation training courses alongside an expert speaker trainer, Olivia Schofield. With the permission of her training group, I performed my talk in front of them. I say "performed" but it was more like "read out aloud".

You see, according to the strict TED process Jane and Harrison had instructed us to follow, we were required to recite the entire script word for word. Parrot-fashion is something I have never asked the people I've trained to do. I've always found that speakers who aren't trained actors can get hung up on memorising scripts. Memorised speeches can often lack freshness, authenticity, and a sense of spontaneity. But I'd agreed to go along with the TEDxBasel process and adhere to it, so I would.

My audience gave me some valuable points of feedback. Olivia then reviewed my script and did something that transformed my ramblings into sharpened prose: she took a red pen and ruthlessly struck out every unnecessary word or phrase. It gave the words space and drama.

Here's an example, from my opening lines:

Before...

I was at BBC Television Centre in London. They used to call it the concrete doughnut. A big, grey sixties building that dominated Shepherd's Bush. The studio lights were about to go up on a prestigious TV debate show. I had always wanted to be on the telly, ever since I was a child. I was in my suit and tie feeling really important, sweating with nerves and anxiety, sitting... in the audience, watching.

After...

BBC Television Centre, London. The studio lights dimmed on a prestigious TV debate show. I was in my suit and tie feeling really important, sweating with nerves and anxiety, sitting... in the audience.

Now my speech was really getting into shape. It was shorter, sharper, and stronger. I'd been lucky enough to have had feedback from some of the world's finest presentation trainers: Olivia had passed it to a couple of trainers she works with and they had provided some excellent guidance.

CHAPTER 3

Foreplay

N ow I was ready to try it out in front of the all-important decision-makers of TEDxBasel. According to our schedule, this was the final rehearsal at which we would be allowed to read from a script.

When I arrived at the meeting venue that was commandeered from another of Basel's companies, the room was already strewn with half-eaten pizzas. Three of my fellow speakers were there, two of whom had already rehearsed in front of Jane, Harrison, and a couple of the other volunteers, including my coach, Martin.

I'd arrived in time to hear the rehearsal of a stand-up comic based in Zurich. I was immediately mesmerised by him, given the size of his ample biceps. His amusing routine was promptly mauled by Harrison and Jane, who told him it belonged in a late-night comedy club and was wholly inappropriate for a TEDx audience. Rather than re-work his script then, they told him they would work on it with him another time so that they could fit in my rehearsal.

I belted out the latest version of my script, confident with how it had progressed.

"Far too loud... too much energy", came the feedback from Harrison.

I had clearly been too confident with my content. You will recall that the topic of my talk was about corporate jargon, commonly referred to in the business world as *bullshit*. My talk had included the use of this word, but only in the correct context. I've always taught my children only to use swear words when absolutely necessary; otherwise, they lose their impact and we'd have nothing left to use when we're next sewing on a button or fitting a new toilet seat.

"Next time, could you try it without using the word *bullshit*?", asked Jane.

"Can I ask why?", I enquired.

"Well, we are both teachers and we like to show the talks to our classes afterwards. If you use that word, we can't show it. Besides that, when your talk is published online, you will miss out on hits from American audiences", she answered.

"But my talk is about bullshit. It would seem odd not to name it. And I wrote it for an audience of adults, not schoolchildren."

"Just try saying *B.S.* instead. It'll be just the same", she insisted.

Harrison then proceeded to take us through the importance of memorising our speeches word-for-word. He did this by reading out the words on a PowerPoint presentation from one of the standard slide decks that TEDx organisers appear to be issued with.

I chose to continue trusting their process, even though I knew that memorising scripts hasn't been a strong point for me in the past. Otherwise, I might've considered going into acting.

At the final dress rehearsal for the organisers, back up in the industrial setting where we'd had our first speakers' meeting, I'd *almost* got the whole 11 minutes memorised. But almost isn't good enough when you're delivering a speech, and like all the other speakers who rehearsed that night, I found myself stumbling over familiar, memory-blocking phrases.

I wasn't yet at the "happy birthday" stage, as Harrison called it: the point where you can recite your speech while you're doing something else, like the washing up, just like everyone can sing "happy birthday" the whole way through while cooking eggs. Even men.

I'd replaced the bullshit word with alternatives wherever it made sense and left just one for the desired impact.

"You're in good shape", came the comment from Jane. "But I'd still like you to try it without *that* word, and see if it works. I don't think it will lose anything."

She hadn't made a murmur when the previous speaker's Italian accent had made the pronunciation of Immanuel Kant's surname sound like something even more offensive.

In the week leading up to The Big Day, I was rehearsing with anyone who would listen: fellow trainers, training groups, other colleagues, friends via FaceTime, myself in the car, my children. My ten-year-old daughter helped me to remember the words by visualising parts of the speech with actions. Her way of demonstrating the phrase "helicopter view" was quite comical.

I rehearsed with an old friend, Matthew, via Skype. He gave me a scathing review, which hurt. This reaction surprised me because by this point I was sure I had a winning speech. In what must have been an "ignore-it-and-it'll-go-away" self-defence mechanism, I promptly blocked out his comments.

Lucy Kellaway, the former *Financial Times* columnist, said in an article referring to her TEDx talk, "all the faffing and rehearsing that TED demands had the effect of making me a cheesy, stilted version of myself." I was blind to the fact that this was happening to me.

The following day my good friend and fellow trainer, O'Patrick Wilson, made me listen to my own speech for me to really hear myself, and he pointed out my "poppy seed".

"This is not you", he told me. "Peter, I know you too well and what's coming out now is just not you. It's not natural. This whole thing has somehow undermined your confidence."

He was right. With all the pressure I'd put on myself and with the strict TED process, I'd become a "cheesy, stilted version of myself", just as Kellaway found.

Memorising the speech word for word was becoming a big stumbling block for me, particularly with a script that had other people's words infringing upon my own. It was at those points where I was encountering difficulty: the places where other people had put words in my mouth.

There was nothing else for it. I had to make the words my own. With only two days to go, I forfeited the speakers' dinner to go through my talk again with O'Patrick. O'Patrick is an excellent trainer who wasn't afraid to push me hard, as all good trainers should. We stripped out the stumbling blocks one by one and, thanks to his partner, Kirsty, added the finishing touch to the talk's punchline.

After almost six months of preparation, finally I felt ready.

The technical rehearsal at the venue itself – the Musical Theatre in Basel – was when it all became real. Having graced the stage on many occasions in the past as part of my work, I knew what to expect and the details I should look out for.

I stood in the centre of the famous TED red carpet and scoped out my stage space. Much to Jane's obvious irritation, I insisted on having a confidence monitor (where the speaker can see what's projected on the screen while facing the audience) installed at the foot of the stage so that I could read the projected examples I would show. These were far too complex for me to memorise. I also insisted on having a stool at the side of the stage from where I could pick up the slide advancer rather than having to hold this rather large device all the way through my speech.

The night before The Big Day, my 15-year-old son, Eric, who would be accompanying me to the event, endured six recitals: three times with "B.S." instead of "bullshit" and three times with "bullshit" uttered once, in the right place.

"There's only one thing for it Dad", said Eric. "You're going to have to say bullshit tomorrow."

And so I did.

CHAPTER 4

Climax

We've already established that I'm one of those freaks who come alive in front of a big audience. The bigger the better as far as I'm concerned. Perhaps it's that yearning for fame thing again. Looking out from the stage into the glare of 700 pairs of eyes, I was in my element.

Basel is a relatively small city home to a handful of large companies. Having worked for two of them in the 16 years I'd spent in the city, I knew many faces in the audience, which spurred me on even more.

The adrenaline kicked in and I felt a satisfying glow as I delivered my speech, "happy birthday" style. I stumbled in a couple of places, but picked up immediately and even managed to play with the crowd in a few places – something that Jane had advised me not to do because it "will isolate the audience that watches it online afterwards". The live audience didn't seem to be bothered by that, as they gave my talk the loudest laughs and applause of the entire event.

I've learned over the years that the single most important thing about making any speech or presentation is to always think about the audience first. In this case, with 700 people each paying 50 Swiss francs to attend the event, they *had* to come first. If I could excite and move them, surely it would carry over to anybody watching online too.

Unbeknownst to the speakers until the day of the event itself, Harrison had appointed himself Master of Ceremonies. If you've ever experienced a Swiss audience, you'll know that they aren't the most outgoing.

The last production I'd seen at the Musical Theatre was The Rocky Horror Show, famous for its audience members dressing up as the cast and joining in with the action.

My husband and I turned out to be virtually the only people dressed in fishnet stockings and suspender belts. Everyone else was in their smart Sunday outfits.

A Swiss audience needs help warming up and Harrison appeared to be doing the opposite. One trainer I work with says: "Some people walk into a room and light it up. Others walk out of a room and light it up".

Despite this – and some of the sessions running way over time, which resulted in a reduced audience for the final session – it seemed to me that people enjoyed the event overall. Being continuously mobbed by "fans" introducing themselves to me, I basked in the glory of being a TEDx star at the drinks reception that followed. My mobile phone was buzzing with messages from friends who had been in the audience or watched the live-streamed event on the internet. As the stage was being dismantled, the organisers, volunteers, and speakers raised a glass together to congratulate each other for a job well done.

Even the discovery, just before I went on stage, that there had been a mistake with my billing in the printed programme (they had printed another speaker's biography in place of mine), could not dampen this moment for me.

CHAPTER 5

Afterglow

This feeling carried on the following week at work. On Monday the head of my department congratulated me personally for "a great speech", as did the Chief Financial Officer when I bumped into him in the lift. Working for one of the largest companies in Europe, this was quite something. Neither had seen it themselves but word had spread in this small city. The CFO told me his wife and daughter had been in the audience and said my talk was the best of the day. The mutual back-patting continued online over the following days between the speakers and event organisers.

A former boss and good friend of mine, Marty Hirsch, told me that even his hairdresser had commented about my talk to him: "He said you were just what the audience needed at the time you came on. Apparently, there had been a bit of a lull. He said you were charismatic, hilarious, spot on, and brilliant! He said you had the capacity crowd in your hand."

Once the euphoria of the TEDx event had subsided, along came the excitement of seeing our talks online, on the official TEDx YouTube channel. This is where any speaker who dreams of fame can have their dreams fulfilled potentially with views in the millions.

The only time I had experienced views in the millions was back in the late eighties when I had appeared on live TV across the UK while co-hosting a young gardeners' slot on BBC1's lunchtime magazine programme, *Daytime Live*. In those days, with only four channels to choose from, TV programmes regularly had viewing figures of over five million, even at lunchtime. My mother was so proud. My schoolmates hated me.

TEDxBasel speakers had been told to expect to wait up to six weeks before videos of our talks could be edited and uploaded onto the YouTube channel. In my impatience to share my talk with family back in the UK, I obtained a download of the live-streamed version from an acquaintance who knows how to do that kind of thing.

A month passed and there was excitement building up amongst the speakers. We'd had little word from the organisers but there was a rumour that some of the talks would be uploaded in the next couple of weeks.

It was not until the beginning of July that I was contacted by Harrison, asking if he and Jane could meet with me to discuss my talk. When we met in the café at the top of Switzerland's tallest building, I was relaxed in giving them my candid feedback about the event: what I thought worked well as a speaker and what could be improved for next time.

I knew that my friend O'Patrick had also given them his feedback as an audience member and TED enthusiast. Having been to other TED events, he wanted to offer some suggestions. Always fair in his assessments, he had even drawn up one of his "mind-maps" showing what he thought worked well and how the event could be improved in the future. When Jane asked, he had shared with them how he'd witnessed my experience as a speaker: he knows me better than most, as we've worked closely together for 15 years.

In the café, I sensed an abrupt change in the conversation when we spoke about the experience I'd had through the process. I felt Jane and Harrison were about to land something big on me. They did.

"We are going to edit out the section where you said *bullshit*", Harrison announced.

"Do I have a say in the matter?", I asked.

"No", said Jane sharply. "It's not negotiable."

Again they cited the reasons of showing it to their classes at school and losing views from American audiences. I was clearly not satisfied with this and asked them to reconsider. Jane was adamant, while Harrison suggested we all sleep on the matter. We parted amicably but I left with a sense of discord emerging. Jane seemingly wasn't happy that I had disobeyed her on The Big Day and used *that word* without her permission on *her* stage.

I followed up immediately with an e-mail – as I'm wont to do – in the hope that they would reconsider:

Good to see you both today, hope you enjoyed the tower view.

I hope we were able to shed light on the perceptions and emotions surrounding O'Patrick's comments. He was only saying what he saw, even if I didn't see what he saw in the thick of things. And I really did appreciate all the work you put in.

I'd ask you to please sleep on the censorship issue. I really would not be happy to lose THAT word. Rory Sutherland [another TED speaker] *used the word "shite" in his TED talk and still got 2.7 million views...*

Best wishes,

Peter

I slept on the matter and the next day I thought I would offer a compromise: a bleep. That should please everyone. I sent off another e-mail that morning:

Dear Jane, Harrison,

I have reflected on our conversation yesterday regarding my use of "that word".

I certainly don't regret using it on the day and if we did it all over again tomorrow, I would use it again. As I explained to you yesterday, I certainly didn't disregard your advice not to use it. I tried not using it in my many rehearsals and for me, it just didn't work as well. So I had to use it on the day for the desired impact. Once. I make no apologies for that.

My TED talk was written for adults and not with an audience of children in mind. I think that the next time you invite speakers, if you want us to design our talk for children, then perhaps the outcome would be slightly different. I also don't agree with your point about American audiences. They are adults too, and if they don't like the use of that word, they can turn it off and watch something else. Something with people shooting each other perhaps.

What I do object to strongly is the heavy-handed use of censorship of something like this when representing an organisation that promotes the spread of ideas. I find it totally contrary to the spirit of TED itself.

However, I do concede that you have the ultimate decision and, as you told me in no uncertain terms yesterday, that is "not negotiable".

I would still like my idea to spread, which was my original intention when first getting involved. So I am willing to allow you to bleep out the "shit". Not the "bull", just the "shit". Please use a bleep, not an edit. By doing this, the impact is not reduced too significantly and you could still play it to a child. I look forward to seeing the final video published very soon I hope.

All the best
Peter

On reflection, my comment about watching something with people shooting each other was somewhat inappropriate, but my point was that there are far worse things that anyone can watch at the click of a mouse than someone saying the word "bullshit" in a TED talk. Indeed, President Trump hasn't been prudish with his choice of words since entering office.

CHAPTER 6

Bombshell

A month passed before I heard any word back from them. Fellow speakers were getting anxious and I'd learned from one that her talk was about to be uploaded to the TEDxBasel website in the coming days. Apparently there had been hold-ups in the editing process.

Then one morning, sitting at my desk in the tallest building in Switzerland, an e-mail arrived from Jane that hit me like a brick.

She began by saying it made her sad that we couldn't find agreement on the matter, and stated that my talk would not be posted at that time. She stressed that it had been a difficult decision and more time would not be invested to revisit it.

She then stated that I was a "poor ambassador" for TEDxBasel and I had not appreciated the effort put in to make my talk a success, adding that it was inappropriate to continue endorsing our relationship.

Bizarrely, Jane finished by saying that I gave a great talk, and she was happy to have given me that chance.

You can no doubt imagine how I felt. Six months' work would now never be seen again. I assumed that sharing my experiences with my friend O'Patrick, who then shared his observations with Jane, constituted being a "poor ambassador". There was nothing else I could think of.

Now, you'll have discovered that I am a man of letters. The reason I appeared on the BBC when I was 14 years old was because I wrote to the television presenter, Alan Titchmarsh, and asked to be on his show. You don't get anything unless you ask.

Incensed by this decision, rather than respond to Jane, I decided to write to the Head of TEDx at TED headquarters in New York:

Dear Mr Herratti,
I was a speaker at the TEDxBasel event in Switzerland on 28th May and I have today been informed by the organisers, Jane and Harrison, that my talk will not be published. Considering the tremendous amount of work that I put into this talk as a speaker, this is extremely frustrating and I am disappointed that my idea will be spread no further.
The reason I have been given is that I used the word "bullshit", once, in my talk. Considering that my topic was about corporate bullshit, this word was quite unavoidable. After using it once for the necessary impact, I subsequently used alternatives.
I met with the organisers following the event, who told me that they intended to edit out the line. I asked not for an edit, but would agree to a bleep. They have today informed me that as we could not reach agreement, my talk will not be posted.
I find it incredulous and totally against the principles of TED – the whole reason why I agreed to do the talk – that people like this, who are trusted with the licence for TED-branded events, should be allowed to impose their personal views and exercise such heavy-handed censorship. I wrote my talk for an intelligent TED audience and not for an audience of schoolchildren. In addition, the organisers have refused to release the feedback results from the audience; I have information to suggest that the highest rated talk of the event was mine.
I would be extremely grateful if you could look into this matter with some urgency.
Yours sincerely,
Peter Sandbach

Five days later I received a brief, unsigned response that simply thanked me for being a speaker, apologised that I'd been having trouble with the organisers, but finished by saying that the decision to publish my talk rested with them. He did, however, say that he had contacted the organisers and told them that he would accept a bleep over the word "bullshit".

At the same time, I had written to the other speakers at the event to try and conjure up support. Over the next few days I received messages from several fellow speakers, sharing my outrage at this situation. One of them even said she wished all the speakers could be happy to see their talks online, and that mine not being there would be a shadow on the day.

Another speaker told me that while she supported my position, she did not feel comfortable speaking out about it. It was clear to me that this news must have filled them with the fear that their talks could also be pulled in such a fashion if they spoke up against the organisers.

CHAPTER 7

Let Battle Commence

I thought about where else I could gather support in the hope that Harrison and Jane might change their position. Small towns have their advantages and I happened to know the sponsorship contacts at the two main companies that sponsored the event. I decided to write to them as well, asking for their support.

Still with no word from Jane and Harrison directly, a few days later I received a call from one of the TEDxBasel volunteers, who happened to work in the same building as me. We met for a coffee and she kindly offered to act as a mediator, as she had seen that tempers had flared on both sides. She asked me not to contact anyone else while she attempted to find a mutual agreement.

On her advice, I wrote to Jane:

Dear Jane,

I understand that you met with [TEDxBasel volunteer] *following the conversation I had with her yesterday. She requested a "ceasefire" for a few days while you reconsider your decision, to which I agreed.*

I refute strongly your assertion that I have been a "poor ambassador for TEDxBasel" when I gave you nothing but my full support for the event and encouraged others to do the same. I would be interested to hear on what grounds you make this assertion.

I still await the results of the audience survey, which I have requested from you previously. It would be interesting to see how my talk was received by them, and if the survey shows any compelling reasons not to publish. Other extremely popular TED talks contain language stronger than the word I used, so your view doesn't appear to be shared by TED itself.

As you reconsider your decision, I would like to refer you to the published TEDx rules, which state that event teams must upload videos of every talk.

If you still decide not to publish, I would insist that you provide me with a video of my talk that I can publish myself.

I look forward to hearing from you before Thursday next week.

Regards,

Peter Sandbach

I had checked the TEDx rules on the TED website, which stated that "event teams must upload videos of every talk from their event [...] unless the content is in violation of our content rules." The content rules forbid anything "commercial, no pseudoscience or anything inflammatory from a political or religious perspective". They say nothing about the word "bullshit" or any other profanity for that matter.

The rules also state: "If an organizer chooses to withhold a talk, they are fully responsible for informing TED staff and then for communicating the reasoning of their actions to the speakers."

Two weeks later I finally received an e-mail response from Jane. She said that they had never viewed the situation as a battle, and had no reason to engage in one. She reiterated that she stood by her decision, which she made based on the information she had. Then she finished by saying that TED rules state that third parties are not allowed to publish talks and that permission is required to use other's content and ideas.

I tried several times to call Jane but she didn't pick up my calls or return my messages. So I called Harrison from a landline number he wouldn't have recognised, he answered, somewhat startled, and agreed to meet me.

If it hadn't been clear before, it was now clear to me that they were not going to be particularly open to discussion. They were both teachers, I had disobeyed them, and now I had to be punished.

It was time to take matters into my own hands.

CHAPTER 8

Fighting the Good Fight

While I took a week's holiday and tried to forget this whole business, I sent the download I had of the live-streamed version of my talk to a friend in the film industry who did a couple of nips and tucks to make it look professional. He also blurred out the TED logo on all the shots. At the same time, another friend set up a YouTube channel for me.

On my return, I met with Harrison at a café in Basel. I asked if he wanted a drink and he declined. So I fired away with the three questions I'd prepared:

"Will you publish my talk?"

"No", he replied.

"Why not?"

"Because you broke the rules."

"Your rules", I reminded him, knowing that we were both aware that the TED organisation would have accepted a bleeped bullshit.

"Yes, our rules", he replied. "You broke our rules, you were disloyal, and you were a poor ambassador to TEDxBasel."

My final question: "Is there anything that can happen now to make you reconsider your decision?"

"No", he said firmly.

I stood to leave. "In that case", I told him, "there's nothing left to discuss. One more thing: if you think I've been a poor ambassador for TEDxBasel so far, you ain't seen nothing yet."

I walked away briskly, quivering with frustration and an anger I'd had a difficult job to prevent from turning into a painful punch in the face for this man. After all, I grew up in Winsford, Cheshire, a town in the North of England where it's so rough, every pub has two bouncers on the door throwing people *in*.

But walk away I did, and behind me I heard him call "Peter! Peter! Do I have to warn you?" Firmly biting my lip, I looked straight ahead and carried on walking.

Later that week, I received a mass e-mail from TEDxBasel proudly announcing that the first talks from the event were available on the official YouTube channel. I took a look and they had done an excellent job of seamlessly editing the best shots of the other speakers, without a hesitation, missed word, or stumble in sight.

I decided that now was the time to let the world enjoy my TED talk as well. I sent the YouTube link to my edit of the live-streamed version (minus TED logo) to everyone I knew, accompanied by the message that "due to a disagreement with the TEDxBasel organisers" I had been forced to publish this myself. I published the link on LinkedIn and Facebook. In the first three days, my talk had been viewed more than 3,200 times.

I was overwhelmed by the positive responses I received, many from people I'd not heard from for several years, some from people I'd trained, from fellow trainers, speakers, journalists, and some from business leaders and CEOs I'd worked with.

Once I'd stopped blushing from all the accolades and messages of support, a message arrived that made me stop, think, and remember someone who had greatly influenced me but had lost his battle with cancer several years ago.

The lead story in my talk was about a former boss of mine, Stephen Smith, who had been CEO of a seed company in the UK at the time when the public debate about genetically modified crops was raging. I was his communications person and our company was the only one with genetically modified crops in the ground in the UK at that time. Even though he was a business leader, Stephen had an uncanny way of connecting with people and talking about the science and the issues around this topic on a level that normal folk could understand. It was Stephen who had ignited my passion for plain talking in business and it was my experience with him that featured in my talk.

I knew he had three sons and I wanted to share my talk with them so I sent the link to someone I thought might know them. She told me that she had forwarded my message and I was so pleased that Stephen's sons might receive a reminder of what an inspirational man their father was.

A couple of days later I was touched to receive an e-mail from one of Stephen's sons, Luke. He told me that my talk was a pleasure to watch, despite my Gloucestershire accent needing some work. He wished me luck and signed off with "Godbless", the way Stephen always used to end his phone calls to me in his unmistakable accent.

Someone else I'd worked closely with on the genetically modified crops issue was a brilliant communicator from Canada, Sheena Bethell, who had been based in Basel for many years. Sadly, she also lost her fight with cancer a few years ago.

I received a mail from her husband:

Hi Peter,

I was thinking of Sheena when I saw your talk, as I know she had quite some admiration for Steve Smith...even if his style was quite different from Sheena's! The world still feels a poorer place without them. However, I think it is great that we have the opportunity to continue their legacies, in our own ways. I'm sure they were both smiling, and laughing, with your talk.

Take care,

Brian

The fact that the stories I used in my talk were stirring fond memories of great people among the people they loved made my maverick decision to self-publish all worthwhile.

CHAPTER 9

Rallying the Troops

Meanwhile, a speaker at the previous year's TEDxBasel who had helped me rehearse my talk was appalled by the decision not to publish. She rallied support amongst speakers and volunteers and began an on-line petition to try to persuade the organisers to change their minds.

The petition gathered around 300 signatures and the following reaction from one of the TEDxBasel volunteers:

Great initiative to have the petition! And based on the Basel expats community reaction, it is gathering steam.

I was a volunteer with the speakers' team, but I quit over how Jane and Harrison chose to handle Peter's talk and then the interaction with Peter. Nevertheless, I reached out to them once again to ask them to do the right thing.

Jane and Harrison are nice people and they did put a lot of heart and soul into this, however TEDxBasel has become bigger than they can handle with their experience as educators. I do not think they ever envisioned the consequences of not posting Peter's talk. What I find rather puzzling is that they are convinced that they did/still doing the right thing. I do not know if this is because of their conviction or just that now they need to stick the course.

As someone who put so much time and energy into TEDxBasel, I am heartbroken to see how things turned out. I am definitely spreading the word from my side and happy to see that the video has reached so many views.

In the end if the video is a success, Peter would be vindicated, and the talk will fulfill its purpose: to reach as many people as possible!

This person also wrote:

As someone who grew up in a communist country under a brutal regime, I very much disagree with "Peter did not follow the rules, let's take Peter to the public square and stone him to death."
There were mistakes done on both sides of this issue. At the same time civilized discussion, reasonable arguments and compromise were available to both parties.
TEDxBasel is a community and the two people who hold the license do not represent the Basel moral police and should not endeavour into carrying out retaliation against a speaker for personal gratification.

At the same time, Marty Hirsch, who is an exquisite writer, decided to tackle the topic in a LinkedIn article with the provocative title "Exposing the Tyranny of TEDxBasel", which gained over 4,000 views.

CHAPTER 10

The Empire Strikes Back

I was heartened by the groundswell of support my cause seemed to be gathering. Then, four days after I privately shared the video of my talk via my YouTube channel, I received a "copyright strike" from YouTube, naming TEDxBasel as having lodged the complaint. My talk was promptly removed (YouTube takes contested videos down immediately after a "copyright strike" pending resolution of any dispute).

With my talk taken down from public viewing, I was now receiving requests to see it from people who had been following the unfolding saga on LinkedIn.

Additionally, TEDxBasel had just sent out a bold message to its mailing list proudly proclaiming that "You can now watch all of TEDxBasel 2016" with links to all the beautifully produced and edited videos. All the talks from the event bar one.

The removal of my video from YouTube spurred me on even more. Undeterred, I found another platform on which to publish my talk. One that I thought would be safer in this game of TEDx cat and mouse. So I re-issued the link to my contacts and the re-posted talk gathered a further 800 views in the 24 hours it remained there. The owners of this publishing platform received a legal warning from TEDxBasel and it was duly removed.

It seemed to me that there were no lengths TEDxBasel wasn't prepared to go to prevent my idea from being spread.

To rub salt into my already sore wounds, I was forwarded an invitation that had been sent to all speakers and volunteers at TEDxBasel for a "special viewing" of the videos from the event at a cinema in Basel. Speakers could celebrate the publishing of their videos online by raising a glass of champagne at a photo opportunity at the Tinguely

Fountain, a quirky piece of art next to the theatre in Basel. Clearly, someone had omitted my name from the invitation list. I saw red when I spotted a Facebook post featuring a photograph of my fellow speakers smiling and raising a glass with Jane and Harrison at their exclusive gala screening.

That same week, I was on a business trip to San Francisco. On a Friday night after a long week's work and a couple of more glasses of wine than usual, I was still stewing after the removal of my video. In my fury from my Californian hotel room, I published a Facebook and LinkedIn post I would regret the following morning. In the post, I urged anyone who agreed that my talk should be published to text the word "bullshit" to the mobile phone numbers of the TEDxBasel organisers, and I posted their numbers.

If you've ever done something regrettable through the lens of alcohol, you'll recognise my thoughts upon awakening, fully clothed. I checked my phone and read words of warning from my friends and supporters in the European time zone. You're probably familiar with the "what on earth have you done?" tones. I received a text message from my loyal neighbour in France telling me that he had duly done his texting duty.

Realising that I'd let my anger get the better of me and that this move had the potential to backfire, I promptly deleted the posts.

Still stewing all the way back to Switzerland, on my return I decided to post my talk on my personal Facebook page instead. Less than four hours later, it was again removed as a result of action by TEDxBasel.

CHAPTER 11

The Last Straw

I was coming to the conclusion that no matter where I posted my talk, it would be stifled shortly after. Sensing that my supporters would soon tire of this game of cat and mouse, I decided to try another tactic. As I've worked in communications for more than 22 years, I'm used to working with the press. I spoke to a writer for the *Basler Zeitung*, the main newspaper in Basel, who had become interested in the story by following the updates on LinkedIn. He asked for an interview, which of course I accepted. A couple of weeks later he called me to tell me to watch out for an article on page three the next day. I was thrilled when I read a prominent piece, in German, entitled "So ein Bullshit" ("Such Bullshit!"), giving a light-hearted summation highlighting the ridiculousness of the situation.

Of course I posted a copy of the article on Facebook and LinkedIn.

The following Monday morning at work, I received a call from my company's Chief Compliance Officer. If you've ever worked in a highly-regulated industry, you'll know that a call from the Chief Compliance Officer is rarely good news. He wanted to meet me that afternoon.

My ever-supportive colleague whispered to me from the next desk: "Peter, if I were in your shoes, I'd be shitting my pants right now."

When I walked into the office of the Chief Compliance Officer, he asked: "Peter, you're probably wondering why I've summoned you here". Before I could answer he exclaimed: "well it's B.S.", and slammed a three-inch thick dossier onto the desk, with a copy of page three of the *Basler Zeitung* staring at me from the top.

He told me how he'd had a long phone conversation, that morning, with Harrison, who had called him to complain about my behaviour and demanded the company do something about it. He also informed me that Harrison had reported me to the Basel police alleging that I had "offended" him and Jane.

Knowing me relatively well but being unaware of the strong feelings that had been running high on both sides, the Chief Compliance Officer asked if I could sort this out over a gentlemanly drink with Harrison and insisted that I meet with him to try to put an end to the matter, muttering something about having more important issues to deal with.

I duly called Harrison, telling him "it's time we met", and so we did a couple of days later in the same place I'd had the fruitless conversation with him the last time. I didn't offer a drink this time.

"How do you think we can resolve this matter?", I asked him, as he sat solemn-faced with very little emotion in his eyes.

"What is your goal?", he asked me in response.

"I just want to draw a line under the whole thing", I said. "How can we do that?"

"You can stop breaking the law for a start", he replied.

"And exactly how am I breaking the law?", I asked.

"You know perfectly well", he said.

"What I do know is that you have reported me to the police and to my employer. Do you intend taking this any further?"

To which he replied: "I have no interest in taking this further. I just want you to take down your talk from YouTube, stop posting the video, provide a written apology to Jane for the attack on us, don't encourage people to contact us over this, and I want your assurance that you will not use your talk in the future without our written permission".

A week or so earlier, someone unknown to me had acquired and re-posted a copy of my talk on their own YouTube channel. I explained that I hadn't posted this latest copy so I had no power over that. I also told him that I retain the rights to a speech I wrote and performed.

"You *know* the parts where Jane and I had input. We have the drafts", he said menacingly.

That took me aback. He was claiming rights to a piece of work that was ultimately mine. Indeed he and Jane had provided some input and ideas, but so had many others who had coached me and helped me to shape and rehearse the speech. To claim that he had the rights to my hard work astounded me.

This time I bit my tongue and quietly wrote down his demands. To me, this was clearly a man who had become obsessed and had started to live in his own story.

"We decide what goes in the speeches and we decide what's posted. It's our decision", he said.

At this point I thought it best to leave.

I informed my company's Chief Compliance Officer of our conversation and sent Harrison the following e-mail:

Dear Harrison,

This is to follow up from our meeting yesterday. It's a pity that this whole matter has been blown out of proportion but I am pleased to hear that you have no interest in taking this further with the police or my employer.

For my part, I will not post the video of my TEDxBasel talk publicly on the internet, nor will I encourage anyone to contact you or Jane about the matter. I wish to offer my heartfelt and sincere apologies to Jane.

My intention from the beginning has simply been to have my talk posted online by TEDxBasel.

However, I do not agree to your demand of me not performing my talk in the future. I retain the right to do that.

As you said you have no interest in taking this matter further, I would ask you to withdraw the complaint against me that you have lodged with the police within the next five days. Please let me know if you have not been able to do this and I will engage a solicitor accordingly.

Sincerely,

Peter Sandbach

I wasn't expecting a response and none came.

CHAPTER 12

The Phoenix Rises

You've no doubt gathered by now that I'm not the kind of person who gives up easily when I feel strongly about an injustice. I began racking my brains for ideas of other ways I could get my talk seen. As the anonymously-published video continued picking up views, then at more than 1,700, I knew there must be an appetite for even more.

I remembered that a year or two previously I had met with one of the organisers of nearby TEDxZurich and offered to coach some of her speakers. I looked up the date of the next TEDxZurich event and it was coming up in November! I hastily contacted her, was open in telling her everything that had gone on with TEDxBasel, and asked if I could perform my speech at her upcoming event.

To my delight, she told me that she had been at the Basel event and seen my speech, telling me that it was the best of the day and she'd be delighted to have me speak at TEDxZurich.

A couple of weeks later she confirmed my speaking slot, sent me the rehearsal schedule, and asked me if I could have the video of my Basel talk removed from YouTube to prevent people finding it when the speaker list was published.

Against my instincts but now armed with the knowledge of how to issue a "copyright strike", the anonymous posting of my talk was quietly removed on my instruction to YouTube.

My nerves leading up to this event were as great as they'd been for the Basel performance. I knew this time it had to be better, even though TEDxZurich had told me that the exact same speech would be fine. For me, delivery had to be spot on and even more powerful this time.

So I rehearsed with another of my training groups, with my children, and with my fellow trainers, including Olivia Schofield, who put me through my paces in person. But when I delivered the speech, it didn't seem to be my speech any longer. It represented so much more than just a ten-minute talk. Whenever the now familiar words fell out of my mouth, "happy birthday"-style, I just felt all the baggage and upset that they had brought. Olivia could feel this too.

It was then, in a darkened meeting room, after hours, in the tallest building in Switzerland, that Olivia made me deliver the speech with no words.

"Just feel it", she told me. "Don't speak it, but I want to see all the emotions you are trying to get across in your talk through your body language and your face".

It seemed odd to deliver a ten-minute speech without talking but somehow it worked. I felt the baggage slowly tumble from the 23rd floor.

"Great! Now with the words", she said.

So I did. And when I got to the word "bullshit", I roared it with might, as all the stress and strife of the last few months fell away.

The following day, in a final panic, I emailed the Chair of TEDxZurich to ask her to confirm that everything was fine from her side, that she was fully aware of the situation with TEDxBasel and still happy to have me as a speaker and publish my talk online after the event. She confirmed in writing that that was the case, as I'd requested. Once bitten and all that.

I booked a hotel room in Zurich for the night before the event and bought a new shirt. One of the things I'd noticed from by Basel performance was that my ample belly was fighting to make its stage appearance too.

Now I was ready for TEDxZurich 2016.

Or so I thought.

CHAPTER 13

The Final Blows

A couple of days before the event I received a text message from the Chair of TEDxZurich. In it she said that she hated to be the bearer of bad news but my speaking slot had been withdrawn. I immediately tried to call her and when I finally managed to speak to her in person she explained that one of their board members, who was also a board member of TEDxBasel, had decided to pull rank and pull the plug on my talk "for the good of the TEDx community in Switzerland". She told me that he would call me to discuss his reasons.

I didn't expect him to call me and he didn't. So naturally I followed up with an e-mail to him:

Dear Mr Bucher,

I would be grateful if you could share with me the reason for cancelling at such short notice my talk at Friday's TEDx event in Zurich.

Given the considerable preparation I have already put into the speech, as well as the chance the TEDxZurich audience would have to enjoy a great talk, I would respectfully ask you to reconsider your decision.

Please feel free to call me.

Yours sincerely,

Peter Sandbach

I have still received no response from Urs Bucher to this day.

Friday 11th November came, and having already booked a day off work, I spent a rainy morning in my pyjamas at home watching the live event from Zurich streamed into my kitchen. In my allotted speaking slot was a TED video from the TED Global archives. I removed my "copyright strike" from the anonymous posting of my talk on YouTube.

Over the next few weeks I tried to put all thoughts of TED out of my mind. I knew that if I didn't, it would take its toll on my mental health.

Christmas was around the corner and I had just packed for my final long-haul business trip of the year when I received a note in the post saying there was a letter at the post office I had to sign for. I picked it up and opened it in the taxi on my way to the airport. The letter heading was from the Basel police authorities and amidst the heady legal-German text were the words "TEDxBasel". My heart sank. I'd hoped that this whole dreadful saga was over, but here it came again to kick me in the Zähne (or "teeth", for those of us who find life simply too short to learn German properly).

I tried to decipher the tricky German legal text but couldn't. As I boarded the plane I asked my long-suffering German colleague, who had patiently and supportively been living through this story with me, to read the letter and tell me whether I could sleep on this flight or if I needed to worry.

She said: "Peter, you can sleep. It looks like they went ahead and tried to press charges against you for copyright breach and harassment. But the Basel Authorities have considered the case and quite clearly say that you haven't broken any laws. What's more, this letter says you're the owner of the rights to your speech and free to publish and perform it wherever you like."

I sat back, sipped on my business class gin and tonic, and snored with relief in the knowledge that I'd been vindicated at last. Having had my worries about the support I had in my adoptive home town, sensible Swiss law had prevailed.

That night as I relaxed in my hotel room after a very long flight, I spotted an article on LinkedIn that had been published by one of my fellow TEDxBasel speakers and colleague at the time. It read: "Ten reasons why you should do a TEDx talk". I posted a neutrally-worded comment offering an alternative point of view, to which she responded by promptly deleting the comment and immediately sending me a text message asking me to "keep her out of it".

So much for the TEDx community, I muttered.

CHAPTER 14

Enough Is Enough

You might have thought that the organisers of TEDxBasel, having received the same letter as I had from the Basel police authorities, would have put this whole matter behind them. I had by this time, despite the added TEDxZurich blow.

Yet on the first working day the following year, they sent an e-mail to my company's Chief Compliance Officer.

In it, Harrison told him that I had not been regretful about my behaviour and I wouldn't remove the video of my talk from YouTube (the one that I hadn't posted). He went on to say that the reason he hadn't provided the prosecutor with further information was because I'd written an apology to Jane and given the assurance that I would remove the video.

Then his tone became more menacing as he said in his e-mail that although the prosecutor decided there wasn't enough for a criminal conviction, verbally he had been told that a civil court might provide a different outcome and a criminal conviction could follow if I continued with further actions.

Harrison certainly wasn't afraid of mincing his words with my employer, yet he stressed again that he had no intention of taking matters further and wanted to see an end to the matter.

Next in this mail he said that I had misrepresented myself to TEDxZurich, which was the reason why my invitation to talk was withdrawn by them. He even reiterated his claim that my talk included his ideas, which I didn't have his permission to use, and that I was welcome to adjust my talk to include only my ideas!

I had just about had enough by now. The Chief Compliance Officer had also quite clearly heard enough and invited me to respond to Harrison directly.

So I did:

Dear Harrison,

When we last met you said you had "no interest" in taking the matter about my speech any further. Yet you continued to press charges with the Basel police. I was pleased to read in their letter that no charges will be brought and that the rights of my speech remain with me.

Yesterday I was saddened to learn that you have again contacted my employer. Contrary to the statement in your e-mail that you "only want this to end", it appears that you intend to continue your personal vendetta against me. As such, this is a private matter and should not involve [Chief Compliance Officer], who asked me to copy him on this message.

I must insist that you stop this activity immediately or I will be forced to instruct a solicitor, as well as inform your employer about your intimidating behaviour towards someone who has done nothing illegal.

I also hereby withdraw my previous apology to Jane.

Please address any further correspondence to me in writing at my home address.

Yours sincerely,

Peter Sandbach

The Chief Compliance Officer, whom I copied, questioned the wisdom of withdrawing my previous apology. I told him it was because I was angry and he urged me to call him first before sending anything the next time I felt that way. What a decent chap he is.

Needless to say, I have never received a response to that e-mail. I am under no illusions that the publication of this book might now provoke a response and provide great material for the next volume.

CHAPTER 15

Fame at Last

A month later, I received a redundancy notice from my employer. There were rumours circulating that losing my job was a result of the whole TEDxBasel affair. In truth, I was just one of 19 casualties from our department in this latest round of reorganisations that happen on a regular basis in large companies. Such changes are now so commonplace in large corporations that many of them even hire "change specialists" to cope with this relentless churn. It makes you wonder how they ever manage to get any real work done.

I'd been part of countless reorganisations before, so I knew the score. In my 11 years with the company, I'd had as many managers, (although exquisite writer Marty Hirsch – see foreword of this book – was far and away the best!). This time it just happened to be my turn to be the turkey with a red spot on his head.

Given the situation, and the lack of open positions that interested me, I decided to do something I'd been contemplating for several years: start my own company. I'd been focusing exclusively on communication training for the last five years and discovered it was where my passion lies: helping people to get their message across clearly. Even with the meagre redundancy package offered, I decided to take the plunge and set up *Free Range Communications GmbH* to carry on doing what I'd grown to love, independently.

I'd often spoken with my family about working freelance, and over lunch one day, when I discussed job opportunities I was looking at, my daughter, Patti, interrupted the conversation: "But Daddy, I thought you were going to work *free range*", to howls of cruel laughter from her brother. "I got the word wrong again", she sobbed.

And so Free Range Communications was born.

A few months earlier, I'd been in the lift at work when the doors opened to a stranger who exclaimed: "It's you, isn't it?" To which I replied, "Yes, it certainly is." He told me he recognised me from my TEDx talk and we agreed to meet for coffee. It turned out that Jeff Bateman works for a company that organises corporate events and we discovered that we have a lot in common regarding our approaches. His company has since been the source of the first work for Free Range Communications, sub-contracting me for speaker training and moderation jobs, including for my former employer. And this all on the strength of my TEDx talk.

Despite its ban, I began to notice how influential my TEDx talk has been in helping to start my fledgling business. Unbelievably, I've been getting many referrals as "the guy who did *that* TED talk".

The crowning moment came on my way to a Christmas drink in Basel, a short distance from where I live in a small town across the border in France. There were only a few people on the cross-border bus and I noticed that one lady kept trying to catch my eye. Being British, I awkwardly avoided her glances. Then as the bus reached its final stop she came over to me and said in a French accent: "Really great TED talk! I was one of your supporters". My smile reached from ear to ear as I told her with a blush that she'd made my day. This was a year and a half after the talk itself, and despite the best efforts of TEDxBasel to stifle my words.

After all these years I had finally found international fame, in my own way.

EPILOGUE:
LESSONS LEARNED

SO, WHAT HAVE I LEARNED, about myself and others, from this whole affair? And why did I continue fighting for what I believed to be right, when many people might have just chalked it up to experience and moved on?

If I reflect on the latter question, the short answer is that I'm a bloody-minded Northerner. People from the North of England are never quite content to be told to shut up and accept their lot. My mother always encouraged me to speak up when I thought something was wrong, as she did throughout her life.

I respect the fact that the organisers of TEDxBasel had invested a great deal of their spare time to make the event a success for the (mainly expat) community in Basel. But that didn't give them the right to impose their own views about appropriate language on speakers, who had also invested a great deal of time, energy, and emotion in their talks. I believe that freedom of speech is one of the fundamental rights worth fighting for, even if it involves fighting a mighty brand like TED.

As one of the volunteers I quoted earlier put it:

TEDxBasel is a community and the two people who hold the license do not represent the Basel moral police and should not endeavour into carrying out retaliation against a speaker for personal gratification.

Harrison and Jane had decided to punish me for disobeying them and I wasn't about to roll over and let them get away with it quietly. At the time of writing, my talk is still not available on any official TEDx channels, although the bootleg copy can still be found on YouTube.

I have lost much of the respect I had for the mighty TED organisation itself. I fear that, while it may have been set up with the best intentions and has no doubt been a rich source of inspiration for many people, it is in danger of losing the magic that fuelled its popularity. If more stories like mine emerge, it is at risk of damaging the halo-like brand it has created.

If nothing else, for me this has been an extremely rich learning experience in trust. I've learned to trust my initial instincts about people because they're usually right.

I've learned that when others have something to lose, you can't always count on them to back you up and do what you think is the right thing.

I saw the support of my fellow speakers, with whom I'd gone through the arduous preparation process, drop off one by one as the situation got more confrontational. None of those who supported me in private were prepared to support me in public. On the other hand, there were some unexpected people, including volunteers, who stuck by their own principles and stood by me.

I've learned that the influence of some people isn't as great as they'd have you believe, particularly when they consider fighting a battle that might not serve their own interests.

I've learned that it's always, always best to hold your tongue, or email, or social media post, until you've slept on your emotions. Or at the very least, wait until you're sober.

I've learned to forgive friends who have a human tendency to protect themselves first. Forgiveness is tough and I've by no means mastered it. It's always worth asking: would I have done the same?

I've struggled with this question when asking it about Harrison and Jane. Would I have done the same had I been in their position? More often than not, my answer has been no. Perhaps I need to frame the question differently: would I have done the same if I had the same values as them?

Above all, I've learned that it's only when the going gets tough that you discover who your real friends are. Those who will support you no matter what. Those who will forgive you for your mistakes or moments of madness. These people can often be your harshest critics, but once you know who they are, I've learned to listen to them and appreciate them for only wanting the best for you.

✳ ✳ ✳

So what exactly was all the fuss about?

With a crafty search on YouTube of my name and "TEDx", you will find the bootleg copy of my talk. But if it's been taken down by the time you read this, here's the speech in full. You'll just have to imagine me speaking it. And by the way, the copyright belongs to me.

A CURE FOR CORPORATE JARGON.

A speech conceived, written, memorised, and performed by Peter Sandbach.

BBC Television Centre, London. The studio lights dimmed on a prestigious TV debate show. I was in my suit and tie feeling really important, sweating with nerves and anxiety, sitting... in the audience.

I'd been going over lines that morning, preparing my boss to be grilled on day time television, on the hottest topic of the day, genetically modified crops. You know, the toxic tomatoes and killer corn you read about in the press.

I scoured the morning newspapers for issues that might come up on the show. I'd briefed him as every good PR person should before their boss appears on live TV to millions across the nation.

Stephen Smith had golden hair and rugged good looks – rather like me actually. OK, you need to use your imagination a bit.

He could charm anyone, from ardent environmentalists to pompous politicians.

And he had a Gloucestershire accent like this that made him sound like a typical farmer. As we know, all English farmers speak with an accent like this.

He was in make-up, charming the lady preparing him for camera.

I said "Stephen, there's an article in the Financial Times this morning saying that statistics in the United States have shown that genetically modified crops aren't giving farmers the benefits they had hoped for. If this comes up on the show, say this".

"Right, Peter".

"Just a bit more powder over here love".

The studio lights went up and I was the only one in the audience wearing a suit. At the front were three experts, each of them committed to their cause. They were ready to do battle on today's topic: Frankenstein Foods, as the Daily Mail liked to call them. There was a scientist – you know the type, socks with sandals; a Greenpeace guy – dreadlocks and a faint whiff of marijuana; and Stephen Smith, the head of the company that was supposedly polluting the English countryside with these "evil crops".

The first question from the audience came from a small man at the front: "I read an article saying that statistics have shown genetically modified crops don't work. Is this true?"

This was the question I'd prepared him for this morning. I felt SO good at my job. SO proud.

Stephen got to his feet straight away. "Well" he said, "if you ask me, statistics are a bit like a bikini", and he cupped his hands like this. *Oh no, what is he doing? This isn't what we rehearsed!* "Statistics are a bit like a bikini. The parts you can see are not very interesting. It's the parts that are covered up that are vital."

I slumped in my seat amidst all those housewives, students, activists. I felt like a man who had been fired upon. And possibly fired from my job. I was devastated. How could he?

But to my surprise the audience loved it, it was refreshing. They expected boring jargon and data and they got humour and wit. For the next hour he had them eating out of his hand. He talked a language they understood. He wiped the floor with Mr Greenpeace. Like a dreadlocked mop.

It was at that moment, as I was sat in my suit, tie cutting into my neck, my dull, boring corporate messages under my arm, that I thought: "If people in companies stopped taking themselves so seriously and started talking a language that real people can understand, they would get more people on their side."

Stephen was convinced of the benefits of genetically modified crops. But too often, those of us who believe in what we are doing take ourselves far too seriously. We get tied up in our own jargon and end up talking absolute nonsense.

How many of us waste much of our lives in boring meetings, listening to self-important people droning on in gobbledegook?

We want to engage our people to innovate, underpinned by thinking outside the box. We want to be a game-changer. To move the needle and shift the paradigm. To take a helicopter view while we drink from the fire hose. We push the envelope and go out of our comfort zone. We transform challenges into opportunities. We deep dive. We create workstreams. We create islands in the stream. We put the fish on the table and the elephant in the room. We even peel back the onion as we penetrate our new normal.

At the end of the day, it is what it is, we don't know what we don't know, so we dovetail our synergies and go the extra mile.

It's BULLSHIT, isn't it? It's corporate Tourette's.

I've worked in communications for 21 years (yes, I am older than I look). For those of you who don't know what communications is, it's just like HR, but you've got to be good with people.

I've made my contribution to this avalanche of business balderdash. Is anyone else here guilty?

I thought today I would put you to the test and see if you can tell which business balderdash is real and which is fake.

Here's the first example.

Writing a mission statement is a staple activity of a "team-building offsite meeting". It's a meaningless piece of jargon cobbled together by people who don't like each other but have to pretend to.

Exhibit 1. Mission Statement

We are Catalysts of Global Excellence
We live our values, which are to:
Bring indispensable expertise and a 3-dimensional perspective
Demonstrate courageous voice, acting as change agents, challenging the status quo

---

Real or fake?

This is real in fact. And it didn't take me too long to find.

You can hear the conversation now can't you:

"Occupation?"
"Catalyst of Global Excellence... and part-time change agent."
"Favourite rock group?"
"Status Quo. I find them quite challenging."

I've not named the company to protect anonymity... and my job. But it could be any department in any company.

But what does this really mean, if we boil it down to its essence? Here's a rough translation. They probably just fly around the world giving PowerPoint presentations.

The next one is an internal appointment announcement.

Exhibit 2. Appointment Announcement

In this position, Joe Bloggs will develop a strategic planning approach across all functions that is aligned with existing processes across the company. Further, he will drive a coordinated approach to initiatives that promote functional excellence and organizational development, along with bringing in best practices.

Real or fake?

It is real. Now if you're like me and you really struggle with answering the question: "What do you do for a living Daddy?", then just spare a thought for this guy. I'm positive it's the job description of somebody who is no doubt highly paid to do... well, he probably flies around the world giving PowerPoint presentations.

Just a couple more. It's a statement from a recruitment brochure.

Exhibit 3. Recruitment brochure.

We will commit to professionally synthesize resource-leveling leadership skills so that we may continue to collaboratively foster competitive methods while maintaining the highest standards.

This one is fake. It's from a website called "missionstatementgenerator.com". But it could just as easily be from any HR department, couldn't it?

And the final example. This is from a talk that was being promoted online recently.

Exhibit 4. Title of a business talk

How do you hold the space for newness to emerge?

Believe it or not, this one is real. It's deceiving because it has words that appear normal but are in fact total gibberish. There's no translation for this one. It's new-age business balderdash. Balderdash 2.0.

Thankfully I have discovered an antidote.

It came to me one blustery evening in deepest Norfolk, in the agricultural East of England. Stephen Smith – the Frankenstein Food man – and I addressed a meeting in the village where we were running a trial of our genetically modified sugar beet. I asked him, "Stephen, why are we wasting our time and energy coming here and talking to people who we will never convince?" He said, "Peter, we're not wasting our time. We walked in there as two faceless men in suits from a corporation they don't trust. And we walked out of there as two decent blokes who have genuinely tried to put their point across in a language they can understand."

Now I encourage all of us to stop speaking self-important nonsense and start speaking sense. Take off your bikini so that we can see what's covered up.

And here's what to do.

The antidote to pierce pomposity consists of three simple questions.

Every time you write something you think is important, from a mission statement to a Facebook post, every time you're about to say something you think is important, from a business presentation to a TED talk, pause for a moment and ask yourself these three questions:

So what?

Who cares?

And WTF... Who's The Father?

PART II

and other lessons in public speaking...

What follows is a non-exhaustive collection of tips I've compiled from my years coaxing people to become a public speaking freak like me. Fortunately I've not yet been able to convert anyone who didn't want to be converted, but I hope these hints can help you, freak or no freak.

PUBLIC SPEAKING LESSON 1

Why You?

I f you're asked to speak in public, whether it's making a wedding toast or making a presentation at a team meeting at work, always ask yourself, before even accepting, why you should do it. It sounds simple, but we don't always ask ourselves that question. If you speak, what will be the benefit? Speaking is a high-risk situation, so why put yourself in that position if you're not going to gain anything? You might be one of those strange people like me and enjoy the kick of speaking in public. Some people prefer skiing to risk their necks. But every skier asks themselves the question at the top of the ski run: "Is the thrill of this going to be worth the risk of breaking a leg?" Remember that a great presentation can make a career. A really bad one can tarnish your reputation until you retire. Early.

Here are some simple questions to ask before you even accept a speaking invitation:

Why am I being asked to speak?

What are the positive aspects for me? Can I strengthen my brand or image by speaking?

What can I give the audience?

Am I the right person for this situation and this audience?

Is this the right time?

What am I able to change as a result of speaking?

What are the risks of speaking? What are the risks of not speaking?

I often work with teams who have not bothered to ask themselves these questions. They simply choose the most senior person to speak, or the person who led the project they are presenting. Or they choose the person who is best at delivering presentations. Sometimes it's obvious, but sometimes it pays not to go down the obvious route.

Top trainer O'Patrick Wilson told me about a situation he had when he was working with a team that needed to get approval on an important project. They knew that their team leader was extremely well qualified, very charismatic, and a great presenter. But he was also known for not holding back his strong opinions, so on this occasion he might act as a lightning rod for people on the decision board that might object.

Rather than choose him, the team took the bold decision to instead put a calm, normally introverted scientist into the limelight. She led the bulk of the presentation, taking the decision-makers calmly through the facts, with the team leader contributing only in the question and answer session. The project was approved.

PUBLIC SPEAKING LESSON 2

It's Not About YOU

Get over yourself. Face it: people are primarily concerned about themselves. The audience first cares about what you can do for them. So figure out what that is. Entertaining them, making them laugh, educating them about something, making them money, saving them time, making them feel important.

You only have to watch any celebrity reality show to see that as soon as someone stops giving an audience what they need, they are dropped for someone who does. Harsh but true. Human empathy can only go so far.

Of course it's not always that extreme. Even for stand-up comedians, audiences will usually start off by giving you the benefit of the doubt. They will begin by mirroring your emotions. If you feel comfortable in front of your audience, they will feel comfortable. If you feel nervous, they will feel nervous *for* you. But if you become self-indulgent, their empathy will waiver.

Think of the presentations you hear every day at work. What do you do when someone starts to introduce themselves at the beginning of their presentation and then takes you through their CV for ten minutes? You start doing your emails. You like a photo of a kitten. You peek at what's on the lunch menu. You may even nod off if you've had a big night the evening before.

Even if you've made this same presentation a thousand times, before you reach for the PowerPoint slides, always take time to consider the following:

Who will be in the audience?

How well do you know them?

What do they care about and what might be on their minds right now?

What couldn't they care less about?

What do they need from you?

How can you give them what they need, or at least go some way to addressing their needs?

What do you want to give them? Do you want to inform, educate, inspire, or entertain them?

For those very important situations – the ones that can make or break a career – it's well worth spending ample time on these questions. If there are powerful decision-makers in the audience, you might consider doing extensive research and a full assessment for each one. But be careful not to focus on one audience member at the expense of the others in the room. This will have the effect of isolating the very person you're trying to reach.

If your presentation is to help your audience reach a decision, you might want to talk to some of the influential people in the room beforehand to uncover any potential objections and to get them on your side from the start.

A couple of years ago, the head of a branding agency was invited to make a keynote speech in front of 350 communications people from a company that was just in the process of refreshing its brand. A prime opportunity to get business, you would've thought. But with his jam-packed slides and totally irrelevant information, he managed to lose his audience within three minutes. Sitting at the back of the auditorium, I witnessed the shimmer of all the iPhones being taken out. I'd estimate that, by the five-minute mark, 70% of the audience were checking their phones, while the other 30% had left for the loo. He had paid no regard to what his audience was interested in.

PUBLIC SPEAKING
LESSON 3

Be Yourself

You've established why you're speaking and who you're speaking to. This is the nice bit: now you need to figure out what's so good about you and use it to your advantage. Never, ever try to be someone you're not. Never make someone else's presentation even if they pay you. If you're not the expert on a topic, don't present on it. If you know you're not good at jokes, don't tell any. Humour is fine, but make it match what you want your own personal brand to be.

What are your own strengths? Write them down. If you're nerdy about a particular subject, how can you use that to make yourself shine?

Think about what gives you confidence and what depletes your confidence. How can you use these points to make sure you show your best?

Audiences are not stupid. They can see when you're being true to yourself. Equally, they can see when you're not. I'm sure we've all seen presentations made by managers delivering messages they don't believe in. They've just been sent some slides that they need to "cascade". It's astounding that this still happens in many companies. It demonstrates a total lack of respect for employees, yet it still happens. The best leaders are the ones who put the slides aside and have a frank conversation with their team members, sharing their real opinions.

Over the years, I've worked with hundreds of scientists who need to present their work but are cautious about making it into "too much of a show". "The science will speak for itself", they tell me. My response is always that sometimes they need to give it a helping hand. That doesn't mean dressing it up to be something it's not or distorting the facts. It does mean bringing it alive with genuine enthusiasm that the audience can share.

PUBLIC SPEAKING
LESSON 4

Always Be Prepared

There's always something more important to do than prepare for a presentation or speech. Let's not kid ourselves, nobody enjoys doing it. Wouldn't it be great if we could just show up and shine? The truth is that even the most professional speakers who make it look effortless put a lot of effort into making it look that way.

If you put the time into crafting your message so it's right for your audience, this will be time well spent. What do you really want to say? Can you boil it down to one memorable and understandable sentence? Have you bothered to test it with other people to make sure it's meaningful? You might think that you're right, that you're the one who knows the most about your subject, but we all have blind spots, things we haven't considered.

Once you have boiled down your message, speak it out loud. Does it sound as good coming from your mouth as it looks on paper?

If you're making an important presentation at work, there's no excuse for not being ready for the tough questions. Imagine you're a journalist pulling apart the presentation. What are the five questions you, as the presenter, would least like to be asked and how will you answer them? Often it's best to address any obvious sticking points up front in your main presentation. It shows you have confidence in what you're talking about and that you've thought about what any objections might be.

Rehearse.

I can't stress this enough. In too many cases, I see people delivering presentations for the first time in front of their real audience! In actual fact, what their audience is witnessing is their *rehearsal*. Too often, some people's idea of rehearsing is to "send the slides round for review".

Rehearse: with your loved ones or your close colleagues, the ones you know will give you frank feedback.

PUBLIC SPEAKING LESSON 5

Don't Be a PowerPoint Slave

I shudder every time I think about how much expensive management time is spent doing PowerPoint slides. I know one senior manager who only got where he is today because he "does great slides". While that's one strategy for success, I know that's not what I'd like as my epitaph.

Many times, I hear from people things like: "But we need to submit the slides in advance" or "they gave us a slide template we need to use". No! If you need to send slides in advance, what's the point in presenting them? People can just read the slides and not waste your or their time being there. One way round this is to only show the important slides about the things they care about and leave out the rest. They already have them anyway and you can pull up a specific slide if they ask a question about it. "Pre-reads", or materials sent ahead of a meeting, are infuriating enough for the attendees of a meeting, so just think how annoyed your audience will be if you insist on reading out the same stuff they've already received. Keep dull details to the pre-reads and the really interesting material for your presentation.

Once you've figured out what you want to say and what they want to know, then you can work out whether any slides are necessary. In many cases they're not. Slides should reinforce what you say, make it stronger or more visual. Use bold images that will stick in people's minds. If necessary, make two sets of slides: one set for "submitting in advance" and one set for presenting. Too often, PowerPoint is used as a way to list information rather than as a visual aid for presenters. Put the information into the notes pages and keep the slides solely for visuals.

If there's a part of your presentation where you don't need a slide, blank the screen. Or insert a blank slide. That way the focus of the audience will be on you and not a slide on something they've just heard.

Some people have said to me: "But if I don't come with slides, people will think I'm not prepared." No they won't! They will be relieved! Use as few slides as possible and make them visual. As long as you've prepared well and thought about what you're going to say, they will see it. Audiences are not stupid.

Over the past five years, I've worked with a CEO on his annual speech to a meeting of the top 200 people in his organisation. This is an important rallying call to his troops, so the first time, I managed to persuade him to use no slides and begin by telling a powerful story. For someone who had previously presented to a backdrop of PowerPoint slides packed with figures and charts, this was quite a leap. But he had the courage to try it and he saw the difference it made. His people were yearning to see the real him, and he certainly delivered. When I sat down with him the last time to begin planning his speech, he greeted me with "Peter, no slides, right?" This year was his best performance yet and the feedback he received was tremendous. His speech created a real buzz that lasted beyond the meeting itself.

PUBLIC SPEAKING LESSON 6

Give Yourself a Chance

We all have good days and bad days. Shit happens. We're all human. Everything that happens to us affects our mood. The weather, the traffic, our families, our pets, our health. TEDxBasel. When we show up to speak, there could be any number of things outside of our control that impact our emotional state. This will affect how you speak and what your audience will feel from you.

Give yourself a chance. Take control of the things you can control before you speak. Get there early. Take the train rather than drive. Don't arrange meetings immediately before (or after) you speak. If you're like me and you know your brain doesn't start working before 10am, don't agree to speak before then if possible. Change your dental appointment. Don't get blind drunk the night before.

If at all possible, check out the room you'll be presenting in.

Here's a checklist:

If you have slides, do they work on their system?

If you have videos, do they play?

How is the sound quality when you speak?

If you need a microphone, can you test it? (Headsets are usually better than a handheld microphone.)

Is there a podium? (If so, make sure you're not stuck behind it – never create barriers between you and your audience.)

Is there water on hand in case you get a frog in your throat?

Is the projector shining in your eyeline? (If it is, make marks on the floor with tape so you know where the no-walk zone is.)

Many of these things might seem obvious, but how many times do we fail to consider the impact an external factor might have on how we show up in front of an audience?

I once insisted that one of my trainees rehearse his entire presentation without any slides. Reluctantly he did. Two weeks later, when he'd delivered his presentation, he thanked me. He told me that he'd turned up at the venue and just before he was due to make his presentation, he gave the technician his memory stick with his slides and none of the fonts worked on their system. Coolly, and in front of the audience who had witnessed this, he went ahead and presented without slides. Now they were doubly impressed.

PUBLIC SPEAKING
LESSON 7

Build a Connection

You've figured out what your audience needs and how you can satisfy them. You're already half way there. Now you need to work out how to get them involved right from the start. Open with a punch. My fellow trainers always make the point that if you don't grab your audience from the start, you can forget the rest because people have already turned their minds to other, more interesting things and all your hard work is wasted. If you are following another speaker, remember that the audience has a choice at that point: Olivia Schofield calls this "the loo or you moment": when the audience are considering taking a break in between speakers, it's the loo or you. Or at the very least the home button on their phone can open up limitless, infinitely more interesting possibilities.

Never start with "good morning" or "thank you" or "welcome". You can hold that until after your punchy opening, even if it's only one line away.

There are some examples of TED talks with great openings. Ric Elias (http://www.ted.com/talks/ric_elias) jumps straight into the action part of the story using visuals, sounds and even smells. Bruce Aylward (https://www.ted.com/talks/bruce_aylward_how_we_ll_stop_polio) asks the audience to do something (close their eyes) and think, flatters them, and uses a prop. Being controversial is another way of grabbing attention at the start. Hans Roslin (http://www.ted.com/talks/hans_rosling_religions_and_babies) does it masterfully with his audience in Doha.

Make sure you keep the connection all the way through. Your audience must be either thinking, feeling, or doing something throughout your speech or presentation. Here are some ways to build a connection so you have them eating out of your hand and to give yourself confidence early on:

Use humour to make them laugh. Never make fun of people in the audience; rather, make fun of yourself. If you're British, like me, this comes naturally. Only use edgy humour if you're sure you can pull it off. But don't use humour if you know you're not naturally good at it. Better to be yourself.

Ask the audience a question. Make sure it's relevant to what you're talking about. If it's a rhetorical question, don't leave too much time before you make that clear or you'll get either an awkward silence or an answer you don't want.

Involve people in the audience. If you know people in the audience, call them out: "I was saying to John earlier today..." or "I heard from Mabel that..." or "Bob was telling me the last time we met...". It will make those people feel involved and glow, and the people sitting around them will glow too. If you don't know people in the audience, get there early and have a chat with one or two people before you speak. Remember two or three of their names, where they're sitting and call them out. Get people to agree with you by raising their hand. This will keep them active and involved. Remember always to mirror what you want your audience to do. If you want them to raise their hand, raise your hand: "How many of you have been...?"

Invite your audience to think about or imagine something. *Imagine* is a very powerful word to use but be careful not to overuse it or the audience will feel manipulated. If you ask them to imagine or think about something, leave enough time for them to do so before moving on to your next point.

PUBLIC SPEAKING LESSON 8

Don't Try to Be Too Clever

My TED talk was all about this. Use language that real people can understand. Steer clear of buzzwords. Instead of making you sound clever, they will have the opposite effect. Audiences are not stupid. They will appreciate it if you speak in terms they can relate to rather than abstract jargon.

Here are some actual phrases I heard presenters use in a recent department meeting:

"Accelerating by embracing a new paradigm".

"Strategic inflection point".

"Maintaining the status quo".

"Becoming an agile organization".

"Optimally balancing our key capabilities".

Then came the crowning glory:

"Ideation".

All that in the space of an hour. I could read the audience's reactions simply by looking at their faces. It's not big and it's certainly not clever, so why do so many people in business insist on talking bullshit? The FT writer I mentioned, Lucy Kellaway, is known for handing out an Annual Guff Award for horrible use of language in business.

I've often heard (particularly from scientists) that using simpler words might seem like they are "dumbing things down". Trust me, it's not the case. People will appreciate it if you use ordinary words to replace technical terms or over-used jargon. As one fellow trainer puts it, nobody ever left a presentation saying, "That guy just made it far too simple."

PUBLIC SPEAKING LESSON 9

Tell Stories

This could be the subject of its own book. Stories stir our basic human emotions. They are how we relate to things, how we make sense of things, how we remember things. Lists and facts can only go so far, but wrap them in a story and your speech can create change and certainly leave a lasting impression.

By stories I mean examples that bring the facts to life. That make things relevant to your audience. Your stories can be personal anecdotes or they can be descriptions of how things got to where they are. That's the thing with stories, you can create them how you like.

Always use stories, however small, when you speak. Here are some tips:

Pick stories that are relevant to what you're speaking about. Make sure there is a point, or moral, of the story, and that you make it obvious. I've heard some speakers tell stories just for the sake of doing so, which leaves the audience asking what the point was.

Your stories should be true unless you're using a metaphor or deliberately want to mislead your audience, in which case let them know that's what you've done so they don't feel cheated.

Don't tell them you're going to tell them a story, just tell it. A story can be a powerful opening to a speech or presentation.

Include the things that went wrong. Those are the most interesting parts, and they make your story more credible. Life's not all positive.

Include enough detail to make your story real but not too much detail that will bore people.

Use descriptions and visual language that will help your audience build a picture in their minds.

Keep a bank of stories you can craft, adapt, and pull out to use regularly. Each story can fit several messages or points that you can use on different occasions for different audiences.

PUBLIC SPEAKING LESSON 10

Find Out How You Did

O nly by critically looking at how you did, giving feedback to yourself, and getting feedback from your audience can you ever get better.

You might not want to give out feedback forms after your wedding speech but at the very least you should find one or two people you trust to tell you the following:

What did you like?

What was missing?

What can I do to make it even better next time?

Write all of this down. Too often we focus only on the negative points, but write down the positive points as well. We need to know what we're doing well in order to keep doing it.

Then the next time you're preparing to speak in public, go back to the feedback you wrote down last time and bloody well do something about it.

ABOUT THE AUTHOR

PETER SANDBACH IS THE FOUNDER of Free Range Communications, a Swiss-based communication training company that helps people get their message across to their audience effectively. Previously, as Head of Communication Training for the healthcare company Roche, Peter created the Roche Academy of Business Communications, which provided courses for the company's leaders to improve their communication skills.

Having held senior communications roles at Roche, prior to joining that company Peter was Head of Communication Services at Syngenta, one of the world's biggest agrochemicals and seeds companies. It was there, as Head of Issue Management, that Peter became well-versed in dealing with controversial issues such as pesticides and genetically modified crops.

Before moving from his native England to work in Switzerland in 2001, Peter led biotechnology communications for Novartis UK, where he spearheaded the creation of the first UK industry communication initiative on genetically modified crops.

He began his communications career in 1995 at De Facto Consultants in the UK, the pioneering scientific PR agency that introduced Dolly, the cloned sheep, to the world.

Peter has an honours degree in biology from the University of Durham (UK).

He is the Founding Squire of Ferrette Morris, the only morris dancing side within an 800km radius of Basel, and he is a constant source of embarrassment to his husband, Silvano, and his two children, Eric and Patti.

Printed in Great Britain
by Amazon

18137407R00048